EVERYDAY PROJECT MANAGEMENT

PETER MULRANEY

Copyright © 2016 by Peter Mulraney

All rights reserved.

No part of this book may be reproduced in any form or by any electronic or mechanical means, including information storage and retrieval systems, without written permission from the author, except for the use of brief quotations in a book review.

ISBN: 978-0-6482523-4-4

This edition published 2018.

❀ Created with Vellum

To RJ Adams and Shawn Manaher from bookmarketingtools for their encouragement and support.

CONTENTS

Preface	vii
Project Overview	1
Project Management Framework	3
Everyday Project Management	5
Project Definition	7
Initiate - what am I doing?	10
Plan - how will I do it?	14
Execute - let's do it!	32
Close - it's done	37
Closing early or pulling the pin on a project	39
Managing a project for yourself	41
Managing a project for someone else	43
Overview for event organisers	45
Overview for writers	49
Final thoughts	52
A note from Peter	55
Also by Peter Mulraney	57

PREFACE

Projects involving billions of dollars require serious project management by highly qualified and experienced project managers.

Most of us won't be doing any of that, but that doesn't mean we can't benefit from applying the principles of project management to our everyday work or personal projects.

I was introduced to project management at Adelaide Bank during a manager development program, and undertook formal training in project management with the Australian Taxation Office.

While I was working for those institutions, I didn't get to manage any billion dollar projects, but I did manage or participate in a number of administrative projects, and I applied project management principles in the execution of my duties as both an auditor and as a portfolio manager of audit procedures.

These days, I apply those same project management principles to my writing projects and, with this book, you'll be able to apply them to your projects, too.

Preface

The first project management textbook I studied was a tome of several hundred pages, filled with a lot of terminology which took me a considerable time investment to comprehend.

This is not one of those books.

Despite all the mystique, project management is not all that complicated, even if some projects are. In my experience, most of the stress associated with projects comes from money, time and communication issues. Project management is all about reducing or eliminating those issues.

PROJECT OVERVIEW

The development and management of a project involves a series of logical steps. The steps set out below apply whether you are managing a project for yourself or for someone else, however, the extent of the work required for each step will depend upon the nature of the project.

Concept development

Somebody has a bright idea or sees a possible solution to a problem.

Project definition

The idea or potential solution is described in detail.

Endorsement

The person funding the work, the project owner, authorises the project with a timeframe, budget and reporting regime.

Project manager appointed

The owner of the project appoints someone to manage the project and to report on progress. This step may involve selection and management of a team of project officers.

Project plan

A detailed plan is developed by the project manager, listing all tasks required to complete the project, and assigning each task to a project team member.

Execution

Project outcomes are developed by completion of the tasks in the project plan. May involve testing of outcomes to ensure they meet owner's specifications.

Implementation

Project outcomes go into production.

Post implementation review

Analysis to determine if the project delivered as planned.

Project closure

Process for closing project.

PROJECT MANAGEMENT FRAMEWORK

In simple terms, project management is nothing more than identifying, and then organising into the appropriate order, the activities required to complete a project so that you get the job done.

Successful project management, however, involves a bit more than that, because there are usually a few constraining factors associated with projects. Factors like time and money. People tend to get sensitive around those factors, especially when it's their money you're spending. Of course, these factors also apply to projects you do for yourself.

To make it easy to identify and organise the activities required to complete a project, project managers use a framework composed of four phases: initiate, plan, execute and close.

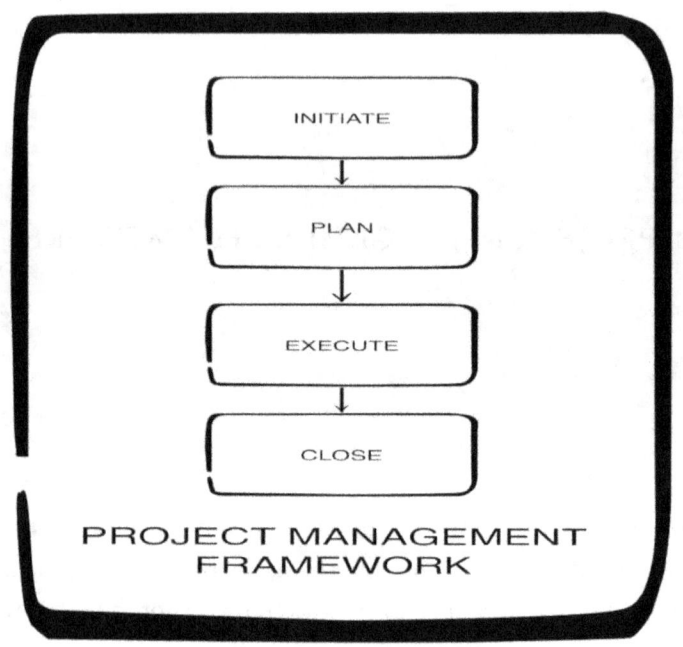

EVERYDAY PROJECT MANAGEMENT

Let's translate the language of that formal project management framework into some words we everyday project managers can understand.

PROJECT DEFINITION

Before you can apply project management principles to a project, someone needs to define what it is you are being asked to manage. In project speak, this is defining the project's scope.

Defining a project is the most important step in the life of a project. It's also the step where many projects are set up for failure, simply due to a lack of detail or a failure to provide a clear description of the desired outcomes.

In large organisations, a project generally doesn't get onto the drawing board until the person proposing it has clearly defined what the project is about, and identified the desired outcomes the project must deliver within defined cost and time constraints. This information is detailed in a document with a name like concept brief, project submission or business specifications. These documents can run into hundreds of pages.

An everyday project needs a similar, if shorter, document. You could use a project on a page document or a simple paragraph detailing the task. Whatever you do, don't take on management of a project without a documented project definition, even if you have to write it yourself, and that includes a project you're doing for yourself.

When defining a project, you need to go beyond a vague definition of what you have in mind. Spell out as much detail as you can about what you're setting out to achieve, and make sure you list any constraining factors, like time and money.

For example, there is no point in stating that you're going to write a book. That could mean anything. You need to detail everything you can about that book.

Let's say you've decided to write a book on project management. You could define your book writing project like this:

I'm writing a book on project management for untrained project managers. I will use a conversation style to introduce project management principles to people interested in improving the management of their small, everyday projects. The book will be in the 12,000 to 15,000 word range, contain simple illustrations, and be published as print on demand and e-book editions. Timeframe for completion: three months.

That's not a very long definition, but it gives the project manager enough information to understand what the project is about. You have defined the task, the intended audience, the style of writing to use, the expected word count, the amount of time allowed for completing the project, and the formats in which the book is to be published.

Another example: let's imagine you've been volunteered to organise a party to celebrate your mother's sixtieth birthday. You might define your party project like this:

I'm organising Mum's sixtieth birthday party on behalf of the family. The celebration is to be held in a city hotel on the day of her birthday, six months from today. Invite her circle of friends in addition to family members. Attendance to be on a pay your own way basis. I and my brothers will fund champagne for the birthday toast, mother's meal and a limo service to transport Mum to and from the venue.

Again, that's not extensive, but it gives you, as the project manager, enough detail to know what has to be done and by when.

More complex tasks simply require a more detailed project definition.

The point of defining a project is for the project owner to provide sufficient information so that, as the project manager, you can understand the task, and agree on the expected outcomes before starting work on the project.

Exercise common sense, but don't accept a project management task without a clearly defined set of expectations - even when you're working for yourself.

INITIATE - WHAT AM I DOING?

This is where a project manager starts work, and your first job is to make sure you understand what it is you have been asked to do. You must understand your task before you begin.

Study the document defining the project. Meet with the project owner and obtain agreement that you have understood the task, and any constraints the owner has imposed.

This is a critical step. There is nothing worse than thinking you have understood the task when you haven't. It is better to be safe than sorry at this point, especially when you are managing work for someone else. This is especially important when you are handed a poorly written project definition or you are given verbal instructions.

If you receive verbal instructions, document your understanding of what you have been asked to do, and verify it with the project owner - before you start work on the project. A little delay at this point can save you major headaches later in the life of the project.

Why is this important? Understanding your task is about getting a clear idea of the expected outcome for the work you are about to undertake. In project management talk, it's about understanding your deliverables - the outcomes you have to deliver. If you don't know what your deliverables are you cannot work out the individual activities required to generate your outcomes.

When you are satisfied that you understand what you are required to deliver, work out the individual activities required to deliver it.

Example 1: project management book project

Definition:

I'm writing a book on project management for untrained project managers. I will use a conversation style to introduce project management principles to people interested in improving the management of their small, everyday projects. The book will be in the 12,000 to 15,000 word range, contain simple illustrations, and be published as print on demand and e-book editions.

Timeframe for completion:

three months.

The deliverable:

a book of between 12,000 and 15,000 words, containing simple illustrations, on project management for untrained project managers. The book is to be written in a conversational style with a focus on managing small everyday projects, and is to be published in two formats: print and e-book.

Constraints:

word count, writing style, illustrations, content focus, formats, time allowed.

Activities required to produce the book.

- Write 12,000 to 15,000 words in conversational style.
- Create illustrations.
- Design cover.
- Editing.
- Generate file for print on demand edition.
- Generate file for e-book edition.
- Upload file to create print on demand edition.
- Upload file to create e-book edition.
- Proofreading.
- Publish.

Note: these are the main activities. Any further breakdown will be identified during development of the plan required to complete these tasks.

Example 2: 60th birthday celebration project

Definition:

I'm organising Mum's sixtieth birthday party on behalf of the family. The celebration is to be held in a city hotel on the day of her birthday, six months from today. Invite her circle of friends in addition to family members. Attendance to be on a pay your own way basis. I and my brothers will fund champagne for the birthday toast, mother's meal and a limo service to transport Mum to and from the venue.

The deliverables:

a birthday party in a city hotel to celebrate mother's sixtieth birthday and a limo service to transport mother to and from the venue.

Constraints:

guest list, date, budget.

Activities required to organise party:

- Establish guest list.
- Select suitable venue.
- Book venue.
- Send invitations.
- Determine number attending.
- Confirm numbers with venue.
- Book limo service.
- Obtain agreed funds from brothers to cover cost of mother's meal, champagne and limo service.

Note: these are the main activities. Any further breakdown will be identified during development of the plan required to complete these tasks.

Summary

Use the statement of the project's definition to determine what you are required to deliver, and to identify any constraints that apply to the project. Then, identify the main activities to be completed in order for you to deliver the required outcomes.

Now, it's time to develop your plan of action.

PLAN - HOW WILL I DO IT?

Before you start work on the doing part, you need to draw up a plan of action that will allow you to deliver your desired outcome - within budget and within the time allowed.

Yeah, I know. You hate planning. You just want to jump straight into doing it. Stop yourself if you get that urge. In the project world, failure to plan really is planning for failure. Been there. Done that. So, there is no need for you to go there.

Planning involves identifying every activity required to complete your task, and then working out the order in which those activities can be completed, how long each activity will take and, more importantly, identifying any activities that are dependent upon the completion of any other activity.

You will find that some activities can be completed at any time, as they are independent components or steps. Others, however, cannot be started until you have completed something else. For example, you can't send your invitations to your mother's sixtieth birthday party until you have booked the venue. (How will the guests know where to go?)

Serious project managers use a tool called a work breakdown structure or WBS. This is a fancy name for a spreadsheet or paper list containing every identified micro activity grouped under a heading for each main activity. Another word you may come across in project management, if you play long enough, is chunking: breaking large things into little bits.

If you're not into spreadsheets, another handy tool is the humble Post-it Note. All you need is a stack of Post-it Notes, a pen, and a wall, whiteboard or window. In fact, Post-it Notes are a good place to start because they're easy to move around as you work out the order of things.

OK, let's see what that might look like.

Example 1: project management book project

Activities required to produce the book:

Write 12,000 to 15,000 words in conversational style

- Set up file in writing application (Scrivener).
- Create outline of topics to cover (Chapter headings).
- Use topic headings to set up Scrivener binder to reflect outline.
- Write content.

Create illustrations

- Determine which application(s) to use for illustrations.
- Determine style of illustrations.
- Determine number of illustrations.
- Determine placement of illustrations.
- Create illustrations for print file.
- Create illustrations for e-book file.

Design cover

- Concept design.
- Select image.
- Format for print.
- Format for e-book.

Editing

- Structural edit.
- Copy edit.
- Graphic edit.

Generate file for print on demand edition

- Generate Word file.
- Format book interior using iStudio Publisher.
- Convert interior file to pdf file.

Generate file for e-book edition

- Generate e-book files (mobi for Kindle and epub for other platforms).
- Preview e-books on e-reader apps.

Upload files to create print on demand edition

- Create book entry on CreateSpace (ISBN required by CreateSpace).
- Upload pdf file for book interior.
- Upload image for cover.

Upload file to create e-book edition

- Create book entry on each platform (ISBN optional on Amazon).
- Upload mobi file and cover image to Amazon.
- Upload epub file and cover image to other platforms.

Proofreading

- Order hardcopy from CreateSpace or download pdf file.
- Proofread hardcopy or print of pdf of interior file.
- Review e-book files using online previewer tools.

Publish

- Authorise publication.

Time allocations

Estimate how long it will take to complete each specific activity in working hours. Unless you've done projects like this before, this will be a best guess, but if you keep track of performance, you can use your knowledge to improve your time estimation in future projects.

Estimates:

- Writing the text - around 30 hours - that's at 500 words an hour.
- Creating the illustrations - around 10 hours.
- Designing the cover - around 1 hour.
- Editing - around 15 hours.
- Creating files for print and e-book versions - 10 minutes.
- Formatting the iStudio Publisher file for the interior of the print edition - about 1 hour.
- Creating the pdf file - 1 minute.

- Uploading the print on demand files - about 1 hour.
- Uploading the e-book files - about 1 hour.
- Proofreading - the online option allows immediate access to the pdf that will be used to print the text, however, proofreading requires examination of a printed hardcopy - 15 hours.
- Publishing - around 10 minutes.

Summing up estimates, it will take about 75 working hours, or 13 six hour days, to complete the project.

Risks - the things that can go wrong

Part of planning for things to go right is being aware of the things that could go wrong with your project, and having a plan to deal with them, if they occur. In project management speak, this is having a risk plan.

If you are working on more than one project or managing a project on top of your normal workload, one risk you need to consider is not getting the time you planned to use on this project. For example; this book project is one of several writing projects I am working on at the same time, which is why I allowed 3 months when I was setting up this project, however, I expect this project to take less than 30 working days to complete.

Another risk you may need to consider is equipment failure. For example; your computer dying on you. Backing up your files to a cloud service, like Dropbox, or to an external drive mitigates the risk of losing all your work.

Order of activities

If you're like me, you'll structure your initial list of activities into a logical sequence based on your experience. That order does not mean, however, that activities must be done in that sequence.

There will be some activities that can be done before preceding activities are complete. For example, writing, illustrating and editing can be done together, however, you can't complete the editing activity until both the writing and illustrating activities are finished.

Critical path and dependencies

Your essential task as project manager, at this point, is to determine dependencies; that is, activities that can't be started until others have been completed. This is known as working out the critical path. In this project, for example, the files to be uploaded, to create the print on demand edition and the e-book edition, cannot be created until the writing, illustrating, editing and cover design activities have been completed. That means those activities must be completed first.

The critical path diagram below illustrates the critical path or order of activities for this project.

Critical Dates

When you have identified the critical path or order in which activities must be completed, work out the date any activity with dependencies must be completed by. This is known as a critical date. Any delay in meeting a critical date will extend the time it takes to complete the project. If you have multiple activities with dependencies, you will have multiple critical dates to meet.

So, how do you work out critical dates? You work backwards using your time estimates within your known working commitments.

For example, this book writing project has a target date for publication: 31 July 2016, and I am working one hour per day on the project. Looking at my time estimates, I'll need about 33 hours to complete the activities dependent on having an illustrated text to edit. That means I need to complete the writing and illustrating activities by 27 June 2016, so that I can complete editing (15 hours) by 12 July 2016, so that I can upload files (2 hours) by 14 July 2016, so that I can complete proofreading (15 hours) by 30 July 2016, and authorise publication of 31 July 2016.

Assigning activities

If you're working alone, you know who will be doing all the activities required to complete the project, unless you choose to outsource activities, like designing the cover.

If you're working with a team or a partner, your final planning activity is to assign activities to the people who will be responsible for completing them.

Project plan

Once you have identified your critical path order of activities and critical dates, draw up a project plan for undertaking the project.

The following diagrams illustrate planning for this project by Post-it Note, critical path mapping, and spreadsheet.

The Post-it Note approach is good for working out the order of activities. It's visual, and it allows you to move things around easily so you can map the critical path. Spreadsheets allow for more detailed planning - once you have worked out your order of activities.

Write
*set up file
*create outline
*topic headings
*daily writing

Illustrations
*style
*number
*placement

Cover
*design
*image
*format

Editing
*structural
*copy
*format

Print file
*format
*convert pdf

e-book
*format
*preview

Uploads
*e-book
*print

Proofread

Publish

Planning by Post-it Note for book project

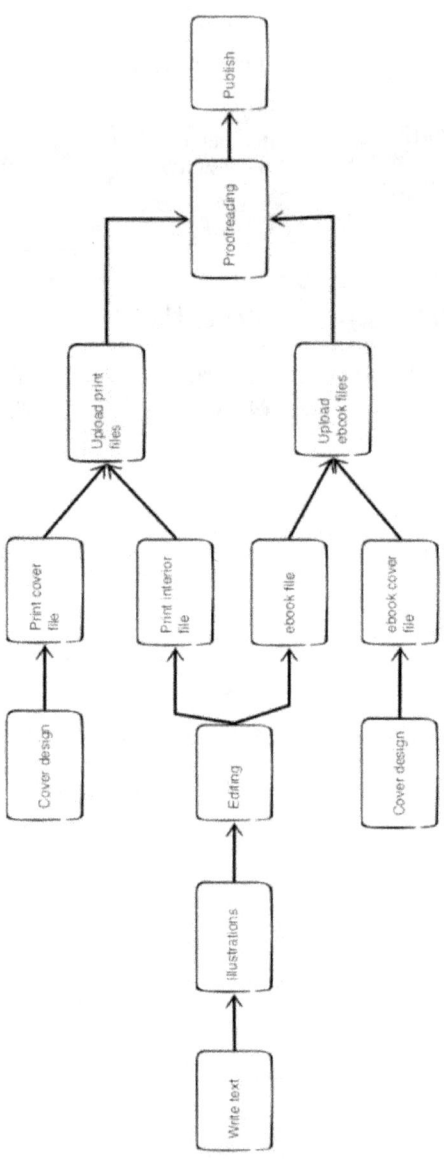

Critical path diagram for book project

Project Plan for:
Everyday Project Management

DATE	ITEM	NOTES	STATUS
4/05/2016	Create Scrivener file	Novel format	Completed
4/05/2016	Write introduction	Refer to OneNote file	Completed
5/05/2016	Write outline	decide scope in terms of size	Completed
9/05/2016	Set up folders in scrivener file	set up targets within Scrinever	Completed
10/05/2016	Write text	Start	In Progress
10/05/2016	Develop illustrations	Start-develop as text requires	In Progress
23/05/2016	Design cover	Consider Post-it Note image	In Progress
27/06/2016	Editing	target date for writing & illustarting	Not started
13/07/2016	Print file	pdf interior & cover image	Not started
13/07/2016	Upload print files		Not started
14/07/2016	Compile ebook files	include cover image	Not started
14/07/2016	Upload ebook files		Not started
15/07/2016	Proofreading		Not started
31/07/2016	Publish		Not started

Planning by spreadsheet for book project

Example 2: 60th birthday celebration

Activities required to organise party:

Establish guest list

- Meet with Mother to determine guest list.
- Draw up guest list.
- Obtain contact details for each guest.
- Research accommodation options available for out-of-town invitees.

Select suitable venue

- Research venues for availability, menu options, and price.
- Select appropriate venue.

Book venue

- Book selected venue.
- Pay any required booking fee or deposit.
- Establish date by which number of diners must be confirmed.

Send invitations

- Determine most appropriate method of delivery.
- Determine desired methods for invitees to respond to invitation.
- Set RSVP date.
- Design invitation.
- Generate invitations.
- Send invitations - include available accommodation details, as required.

Determine number attending

- Collate RSVP responses.

Confirm numbers with venue

- Call venue and confirm numbers.

Book limo service

- Research available services.
- Book appropriate service.
- Pay any required booking fee or deposit.

Obtain agreed funds from brothers to cover cost of mother's meal, champagne and limo service.

- Tally costs based on number of attendees, estimate of Mother's meal cost, and cost of limo service.
- Calculate per brother contribution to cover costs.
- Advise brothers of contribution required and provide bank account details for payment.

Time allocations

Estimate how long it will take to complete each specific activity in working hours. Unless you've done projects like this before, this will be a best guess, but if you keep track of performance, you can use your knowledge to improve your time estimation in future projects. Another thing to keep in mind with a project of this kind is that it's something you will most likely be doing in your non-work hours.

Estimates:

- Establishing guest list - an evening with Mother - 4 hours.
- Research available accommodation - internet search - 1 hour.
- Select suitable venue - internet search and telephone calls - 4 hours.
- Book venue - 10 minutes.
- Invitations - use a template, print and post - 2 hours.
- Collate RSVP information - 10 minutes.

- Confirm booking - 10 minutes.
- Limo service - research and book - 1 hour.
- Calculate and advise brothers of required contribution - 15 minutes.

Summing up estimates, it will take about 12 working hours to complete this project.

Risks - things that can go wrong

Part of planning for things to go right is being aware of the things that could go wrong with your project, and having a plan to deal with them, if they occur. In project management speak, this is having a risk plan.

This particular project looks fairly straightforward. You could knock it off over a weekend - which would probably be a good idea. However, this type of project, where you seem to have plenty of time - your mother's birthday is six months away - comes with some in-built risks, the primary one being failing to act as soon as practicable. The longer you delay taking action will only increase your risk of not being able to book a suitable venue. The best action to mitigate this risk is doing it now.

If you're not particularly skilled when it comes to designing invitations or using computers, consider outsourcing that activity or co-opting an appropriately skilled family member.

The biggest challenge I've encountered with this type of project is getting the correct spelling for people's names and their current contact details. You may need to call on the wider family network - if Mother's address book is not up to date.

Order of activities

If you're like me, you'll structure your initial list of activities into a logical sequence based on your experience. That order does not mean, however, that activities must be done in that sequence. There will be some activities that can be done before preceding activities are complete. For example, you can book the limo service before you write the invitations, however, you can't finalise that booking until you have selected the venue.

Critical path and dependencies

Your essential task as project manager, at this point, is to determine dependencies; that is, activities that can't be started until others have been completed. This is known as working out the critical path. In this project, for example, you would not select the venue until you had some idea how many people will be on the guest list, and you can't send invitations until you have established that guest list and booked the venue.

The critical path diagram below illustrates the critical path or order of activities for this project.

Critical dates

When you have identified the critical path or order in which activities must be completed, work out the date any activity with dependencies must be completed by. This is known as a critical date. Any delay in meeting a critical date will extend the time it takes to complete the project. If you have multiple activities with dependencies, you will have multiple critical dates to meet.

So, how do you work out critical dates? You work backwards, but in this case you also need to consider what is known as **lag or wait time**, that is, the time between one activity ending and the next activity starting. The most obvious lag time to consider will be the period between sending the invitations and advising the venue of the final number of attendees. (You have to wait for people to reply to your invitation.)

In this project, you know the date of the birthday. Booking a suitable venue will be the critical event, as there will be no party without a venue, so you need to determine the date by which this activity must be completed. That date will determine what date the guest list must be finalised. The last date on which you can notify the venue of the final number of people attending will determine the RSVP date, which in turn will determine when you need to send out the invitations so that people will have sufficient time to respond.

Assigning activities

If you're working alone, you know who will be doing all the activities required to complete the project.

If you're working with a team or a partner, your final planning activity is to assign activities to the people who will be responsible for completing them.

Project plan

Once you have identified your critical path order of activities and critical dates, draw up a project plan for undertaking the project.

The following diagrams illustrate planning for this project by Post-it Note, critical path mapping, and spreadsheet.

The Post-it Note approach is good for working out the order of activities. It's visual, and it allows you to move things around easily so you can map the critical path. Spreadsheets allow for more detailed planning - once you have worked out your order of activities.

Everyday Project Management

Guest list
*interview Mother
*current contact details

Venue
*research
*book
*confirm last date

Invitations
*set RSVP
*design
*print
*post

Responses
*collate
*confirm numbers

Limo
*research
*book

Contributions
*calculate
*collect

Planning by Post-it Note for birthday party

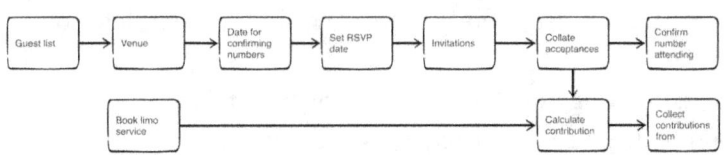

Critical path diagram for birthday party

Project Plan for:
Mum's 60th Birthday Party

DATE	ITEM	NOTES	STATUS
	Establish guest list	Meet with Mother	
	Obtain contact details	Correct spelling/current address	
	Research accommodation options	For out of town guests	
	Research venues	Internet	
	Select venue	Estimate numbers	
	Book venue	Booking fee? Last date for numbers?	
	Design invitations	RSVP date -allow time advise venue	
	Prepare invitations	Guset list	
	Send invitations	post, email etc	
	Collate RSVPs		
	Confirm numbers with venue		
	Research limo service		
	Book limo	Payment arrangements?	
	Obtain contribution from brothers	Covers limo, mother's meal & champagne	

Planning by spreadsheet for birthday party

Summary

Planning is:

- creating a list of the activities required to complete your task,
- estimating how long each activity will take,
- identifying critical activities and critical dates,
- working out the order in which activities need to be completed,
- identifying and addressing risks, and
- assigning responsibility for completing each activity.

When you have your plan, you're ready to start work on the doing.

EXECUTE - LET'S DO IT!

When you have planned what needs to be done, it's time to get down to doing it.

Execution is simply doing what you planned to do to complete the project. In our examples, it's writing the book and arranging the birthday party.

One essential project management skill required during execution is keeping track of things, so that you can ensure the project continues to move towards it's delivery or completion date. This brings us to reporting.

Reporting

In your own projects, reporting is nothing more than crossing off the activities on your Post-it Notes or updating the status of an activity in your spreadsheet. In my project spreadsheets I use: Not Started; In Progress; Waiting; Completed, to show the status of each activity.

Apart from tracking the status of each activity, you also need to keep an eye on your critical dates. You can do this by setting up reminders in your calendar or writing the dates on your Post-it Notes. Another way is to enter a start date and a completed date into your spreadsheet for every activity. The dates I'm using in the spreadsheet for writing this book are the target dates for starting each activity so that I'll meet my critical dates. When I don't start by the date I've entered for an activity, I know I'm behind schedule.

When you are working with others, you need to keep track of their progress on completing the work assigned to them. The easiest way to do that is to meet with them on a regular basis and update your spreadsheet or Post-it Notes during each meeting.

Another aspect you need to consider is keeping track of your costs. If your project has an allocated budget, you need to ensure you don't overspend or run out of money before the work is done.

Reporting takes on an additional significance when you are managing a project for someone else. In addition to keeping track of things, you need to keep the project's owner updated on the progress of the project. This could mean another round of meetings or sending a series of progress reports that let the owner know what's been achieved to date. It's also important to keep your project owner informed of any issues you encounter that may delay the project or require more money.

Another important role of reporting is identifying when it's appropriate to stop working on a project. Let's face it, not every idea turns out to be a good idea, some cost a lot more than anticipated, and others just don't work out for a variety of reasons.

Handling changes

In a perfect world, everything happens according to your plan. In the imperfect world we live in, things change all the time. If you're working on a project for someone else, they may change their mind about some aspect of the project. Of course, this also applies when you change your mind about an aspect of your own project.

Changes can be major or minor. A minor change is something like a tweak to the deliverable that will not impact your time or money constraints. A major change is something that will impact those constraints. Major changes require a renegotiation of the project's deliverable and constraints with the project owner. This means revisiting and updating the project definition document.

A major change will also require a revision of your project plan to ensure you can deliver the revised outcome.

If we consider our birthday party project, adding someone to the guest list would be a minor change. Changing the date of the party or the venue after the invitations had gone out would be a major change.

The best way to manage changes is to have a change management process, which simply means having a method for reviewing any changes with the project owner before going ahead with the change.

Scope creep

This is an ever-present danger in all projects. Scope creep is adding things in that were not required in the original project definition. Some people refer to this as gold plating, that is, going for the best possible outcome, as opposed to the practical outcome you initially agreed to produce, in the belief that you are adding value. Uncontrolled scope creep usually costs time and money. The best way to manage scope creep is to have a change management process. In personal projects, scope creep may be a symptom of procrastination or a warning sign that you're caught in the dream of perfection.

Managing setbacks

Sometimes, things just don't work out. Someone you outsourced a job to lets you down. Your equipment breakdowns or some aspect of your project fails. If you're working with a project team, one of your specialists getting sick can be a major setback, especially if that person cannot be replaced quickly or if the activity the specialist was working on is a critical activity.

This is where your risk plan comes into play. If you have foreseen the setback and have a plan for managing it, go with your plan. If you haven't foreseen a particular setback, you need to find a workaround, and you need to keep the project owner informed.

To give you an example of a setback, in one of my other writing projects I was planning to publish a full color paperback edition of a book I had written, something I hadn't done before. I knew I had to use images with a resolution of 300 dpi (dots per inch), which I duly inserted into my Word document. Then, I discovered that Word was converting those images into 72 dpi images, which is fine for on screen display but not helpful for printing, as the pictures come with dots of color and white spaces. That project came to a halt, until I realised that if others had done it, there had to be a way of doing it, and, of course, there is. In my case, it was a matter of researching affordable desktop publishing applications to discover iStudio Publishing, which exports images to pdf without downsizing their resolution.

Unless you're doing something totally original, someone will have done something like you're doing, and these days there is a good chance the solution to your setback will be available at the end of an internet search, a twitter request for help or an email to a complete stranger.

Implementation

This is the part where you release your idea into the wild. In our examples, this is publishing the book and holding the birthday party. However, your work as project manager is not over, which is why there is one more step to consider: Closing the project.

Summary

Execution is completing the activities in your plan in the correct order, coping with changes and setbacks, tracking progress and keeping the project owner informed. Execution ends when you deliver the required outcome or deliverable.

CLOSE - IT'S DONE

Closing a project or tying up loose ends is often overlooked.

The book's published; the party's over. The temptation is to move on. Resist that temptation for a moment.

In the case of the birthday party, closing could be as simple as making sure you got the money from your brothers, but it could involve filing away your project plan and your invitation template for the next party you have to organise.

In the case of the book, closing involves checking the book's details on each retailer's website, ordering a copy of the paperback and downloading the e-book to your reading device to ensure they are delivering what you published. It also involves storing your files so you can quickly revise and reload them to correct any of those errors that slipped through, despite your best proofreading efforts.

Post implementation review

When you complete a project of a type you are likely to repeat, review how things went, and update your basic project plan for that type of project. This is a good time to compare your time estimates with the actual time it took to complete particular activities, so that your next round of estimates will be better informed. The same applies to costs.

If you're managing everyday projects within a large organisation, closing may also include sharing any insights you gained from completing the project.

Final reporting

For your personal projects, this is simply making sure you have completed every activity.

When you manage a project for someone else, closing involves confirming with the project owner that you delivered what they asked for, and providing a final statement of accounts. They always want to know where the money went, and if there are any unspent funds.

Celebration

Another important thing we often overlook is celebrating our achievements. If you worked on your own, find some way to celebrate or reward yourself for completing the job. If you worked in a team, arrange a social event - something as informal as a morning tea or having lunch together - to celebrate the end of the project.

CLOSING EARLY OR PULLING THE PIN ON A PROJECT

You may have noticed that, despite setting a target of 12,000 to 15,000 words for this book, it doesn't contain that many words. I could have revised all those references to the proposed word count or found some stories to pad out the text, and you'd be none the wiser, so why didn't I do that?

Knowing when to stop work on a project is a skill worth developing.

The text I've written meets my objective for providing you with a project management framework to manage your everyday projects. That means I've delivered my project management book project's outcome.

When you are working on the execution part of your projects, keep asking yourself if you need to keep tweaking or developing, or if you've delivered your outcome. Sometimes, your product doesn't need every bell and whistle you can imagine. Often, it's a better use of your time and money to develop a minimal viable product that will do the job, and move on.

The project management literature is full of stories about projects that went on for too long. Don't let yours become one of them. Have the courage to pull the pin when it becomes obvious that you can't do any more or that your deliverable is no longer required.

MANAGING A PROJECT FOR YOURSELF

Most everyday projects will be personal projects you want to complete for yourself, like organising an event, planning a holiday, buying a new house or writing a book. In these types of projects it's all about you. You're the one who wants the outcome, you're the one doing the planning, and you're the one doing the work.

Sometimes you'll get talked into doing a project for someone else, like organising a workshop for your partner or a celebration for your family, which simply adds another level into your planning and reporting. Before you start work, make sure you have understood what it is your partner or family wants, and that you are aware of any constraints, like time and money, and remember to keep them in the loop as you pull things together for them. That may involve nothing more than a few meetings or phone calls.

If you are self-employed or run a small business, some of your projects will be related to your business goals, and may involve other people working on the project with you. These projects may include tasks that you outsource to third party suppliers or tasks that you allocate to your employees. In these types of projects you need to pay attention to the details and keep track of tasks, otherwise you run the risk of losing control of your delivery date or budget - or both.

MANAGING A PROJECT FOR SOMEONE ELSE

Some everyday projects will be projects you do for your employer or a community organisation.

This is a whole new ball game, when compared to managing projects for yourself. The word to keep in mind is accountability, because you will be held accountable for the outcome, and you may need to hold others accountable for their performance.

When managing a project for someone else, it's essential to establish agreement on the project's deliverables before you start work on the project. In a small organisation or business, you may have to write the project definition document after meeting with your boss. If you do, get the boss to read it, and confirm that you have understood what is required.

Working alone

Some projects will be jobs you take on in addition to your normal duties. Others will be jobs that take you offline while you complete the task. If you are working on your own, you can treat it like a personal project with one main difference: reporting. You need to keep track of your progress and your spending, and keep the boss informed.

Working with others

Project work often involves working as part of a project team. When you are the project manager, not only do you need to manage the project, you also need to manage the project team. This usually means taking on all management responsibility for team members. You need to remember to build this into your project plan, and you need to become aware of any pre-approved leave arrangements for individual team members, and build that into your time estimates.

In small organisations, project teams often come with another challenge. The ideal project situation is to have a team of project officers that reports to you for the duration of the project. Sometimes, due to budget restraints, you end up with a part-time project team, where your project officers report to their normal manager for administrative purposes, like attendance and leave reporting, and only spend a portion of their working hours working for you.

My recommendation, if you find yourself in this situation, is to meet with the manager of each individual, before you start any of the doing work, to agree clear protocols around the hours each project officer will be available for working on your project. Put those protocols in writing, and provide a copy to all managers and project officers involved.

The pressure to perform a person's normal duties often becomes too much for some employees to resist, and that will lead to delays for your project. Better to address it upfront than through confrontation later - after managers let their business needs override yours.

OVERVIEW FOR EVENT ORGANISERS

Many everyday projects involve organising events, like workshops, conferences, training programs, fundraisers, and celebrations. Some will be events that participants pay to attend. Others will be events that you or your organisation provide to employees, the public or family members.

Whether your event is money generating or not, you can apply everyday project management principles to both organising it and running it.

Principle 1: project scope - what am I doing?

Determine what type of event you are organising and the objective for holding the event. This will impact your planning, since not all events are equal. For example, when you are organising an event with a money making objective, you need to pay close attention to costs and pricing. If you are organising a training program to improve a measurable performance outcome, you need to establish a benchmark measure of a key performance indicator. Fundraising events, like charity auctions, often rely on volunteers and donations.

Another vital consideration is the size of the event you are organising. A half day workshop or a one day training program for ten to twenty participants requires a different level of planning than a three day conference catering for 200 participants or a residential training program for twenty participants.

The bigger the event, the more important it is that you have a project definition document describing the objective, and detailing everything to be provided for both presenters and participants. For example, will you arrange accommodation for participants or provide details of accommodation available either at or near the venue? What about catering? What about getting there? You need guidance on these issues before you start, as they impact costs and pricing, and options like arranging accommodation require someone to complete the task, and often a lot of hassles you would be better off leaving to staff at accommodation providers. The same can be said about making travel arrangements.

Principle 2: planning - how will I do it?

Project planning relies on chunking or breaking the job into small manageable steps. Start by creating a list of all the activities you'll need to complete to perform the task described in your project definition. Once you have your list, map the critical path of those activities to get them into the correct order, so that you can calculate all critical dates for completing activities to meet your target date.

One thing all events have in common is a requirement for a venue in which to stage the event. Booking a venue is a critical activity when organising an event, even an in-house training session. Part of booking a venue is negotiating the services you want the venue to provide, for example, food and drinks at breaks, lunch or a conference dinner. You'll also want to determine what facilities the venue has to support your event, for example, microphones and projectors, and you might be able to negotiate a special accommodation rate for conference attendees that you can advertise.

What you do next depends on the type of event you are organising. When you are organising a money making event, your next consideration will be pricing. What are you going to charge participants to attend the event?

The answer to that question will be determined by the anticipated number of participants, all costs associated with the event, including any required insurance cover, that you or your organisation will be responsible for paying, and the amount of money to be raised by the event. This means you have to determine all of the costs associated with the event before you can advertise the event. So, pricing is another critical activity. When setting the price, consider what refund policy will apply if participants cancel after paying. You need to include that in your advertising.

When you're organising an event with a budget, you still need to determine costs as early as possible to ensure you can stage the event without blowing that budget.

If you are engaging external speakers or trainers for your event, determining their availability is another critical event, and you will need a back-up plan to cover the risk of that availability changing. If you're paying for their services, accommodation and travel, this is an extension of determining your costs.

When you are in a position to advertise, you also need a system for accepting bookings and payments.

Another thing to plan for is the development and production of any materials required to stage the event, and arranging for sufficient support people to be on hand during the staging of the event, for example, staff to handle the registration process. In fact, it's probably a good idea to have a separate plan for the actual staging of the event.

Principle 3: execution or doing the tasks - let's do it!

This is the part where you do what you planned. The final part of execution for events is the actual staging of the event.

Principle 4: close - it's done.

Closing an event can be broken into two components: administrative and analysis.

The administrative part is about making sure all accounts have been paid, and all monies collected are accounted for. It may include sending thank you notes, especially for fundraising events that relied on volunteers and donations. It should include filing a copy of your project plan for future reference. It may involve preparing a final report for your project owner.

The analysis component is about working out whether the event met its objectives. Did you raise the money required? Did the training program boost performance according to your key indicator? Did you learn anything you can use to do a better job next time? Did you deliver on time within budget?

The results of your analysis should form the text of your final report, even if it's to yourself.

OVERVIEW FOR WRITERS

Project management principles can be applied to writing a book of any kind, and are even more applicable in this age of independent self-publishing where writers are doing more than simply writing the words.

Principle 1: project scope - what am I doing?

Determine what type of book you are writing, how many words it will contain, when you plan to publish it, and the money available to fund the development and marketing of the book.

Write those things down. In project management speak, this is all about defining your deliverables and setting your budget.

Principle 2: planning - how will I do it?

The secret to project planning is known as chunking. This is breaking down the process, from deciding what to write all the way through to launching the book, into individual tasks.

Once you have identified all the tasks, map out the sequences of tasks and determine their dependencies. That means working out the order in which tasks need to be completed, identifying those tasks that can be done at the same time and those that can't be done until another task has been completed. One of the traps to avoid is linear thinking; that is, thinking you have to write the book before you can do anything else.

Planning is where you start thinking about marketing and audience building tasks, because these activities can be done at the same time as writing.

Another planning activity is to allocate resources to specific tasks. Okay, you know who is doing the writing, and the initial edits, but who are your beta readers? Who is your editor? Who will be doing the cover design? Record the answers to those questions during planning or at least identify them as tasks that need to be completed.

This is also the time for working out how you'll fit everything into your timeline. How many words per day do you need to generate to create that first draft? How much time will you need to edit and revise? When will you need to engage editors, cover designers and beta readers?

In project management speak this is known as developing a work breakdown schedule, and the secret is to break each task into its parts. Editing, for example, is not one task. Consider the structural edit, the copy edit, the format edit. If you intend to publish on multiple platforms, develop a checklist for preparing the file for each platform - so that your file for each platform contains the correct end pages.

Planning is the part where the big boys use MS Project but you can do it using a simpler program, like Excel or Bento, or you can do it with Post-it Notes stuck onto the wall. I like to use Excel because it allows me to move things around, and I can filter tasks into different streams of activity. It also allows me to put a target date next to each task and to record its status: Not started; In progress; Waiting on someone; Completed.

The final planning task is to develop the plan of the book. It's one thing to plan the overall project. It's another step altogether to develop the plan or outline of your book before you move to the actual writing activity.

Principle 3: execution or doing the tasks - let's do it!

Complete each step in your plan. Sounds easy, but this is actually the part that requires the most self-discipline. Execution is where you sit down and write every day, and do all those other things required to develop your author platform, promote your work and build your audience.

This part ends when you publish the book.

Principle 4: close - it's done.

Publication marks the end of the development of your book. The writing is finished. The book has been launched.

Your book will have a life supported by its marketing plan, which you developed as one of your project's tasks, but you need to close the project of its development.

One of the benefits of completing a book-writing project using project management principles is that you'll have a project management framework you can apply to your next writing project. So, before you close your project, conduct a post publication review of what worked and what didn't so that you can tweak your framework for your next book.

FINAL THOUGHTS

You do not need formal project management certification to manage everyday projects. All you need is common sense and a framework, like the everyday project management framework, to work with.

You do not need a formal project to apply project management principles to your work. These principles work for any task that requires the completion of a series of activities.

Project management is simply applying self-discipline to your work habits. It's about taking the time to define what you're setting out to do, and planning how you will do it, before launching into the doing.

You don't need any fancy equipment or software. All you need to get started is a pencil and paper or a pen and Post-it Notes. For most everyday projects, a spreadsheet is about as sophisticated as you need to go for planning and reporting purposes. You can even draw a critical path map in most spreadsheet applications, but the easiest way to construct a critical path map is to use Post-it Notes on a wall or a whiteboard. For those interested, I used the

Diagrammix App to draw the critical path map illustrations in the example projects.

The next time you have an event to organise or a job to complete, pull out this book, and follow the everyday project management framework to get the job done.

A NOTE FROM PETER

Hi, I'm Australia's crime writing mystic, so you might be wondering why I've written a book on project management. Short answer is a desire to share the knowledge I gained from applying project management principles in the workplace, and from using them to organise my writing projects. My hope is you'll be able to apply these everyday project management principles to your projects.

If you found *Everyday Project Management* useful, please consider writing a review or sharing the book's details on social media to help other readers find the book.

In addition to the *Everyday Project Management,* I have several other books you might enjoy reading.

You can find details about all of my books and read my blog on **www.petermulraney.com** and join my **Crime Readers Group** to download a free copy of *Deadly Sands* or subscribe to my monthly newsletter 'Insights from a crime writing mystic' and download a free copy of *A Question of Perspective* and be one of the first to know when my next book will be released.

ALSO BY PETER MULRANEY

Inspector West series

After

The Holiday

Holy Death

Whistleblower

Twisted Justice

The East Park Syndicate

Stella Bruno Investigates series

The Identity Thief

A Gun of Many Parts

Bones in the Forest

A Deadly Game of Hangman

Taken

Fallout

The Identity Thief Collection

The Fallout Collection

Novella

The New Girlfriend

Living Alone series

After She's Gone

Cooking 4 One

Sanity Savers

Living Alone (Collection)

Everyday Business Skills

Everyday Productivity

Everyday Money Management

Writings of the Mystic

Sharing the Journey: Reflections of a Reluctant Mystic

A Question of Perspective

My Life is My Responsibility: Insights for Conscious Living

I Am Affirmations: The Power of Words

Beyond the Words: Reflections on I Am Affirmations

Mystical Journey: A Handbook for Modern Mystics

Sharing the Journey Coloring Books

Mandalas

Mandalas by 3

Sharing the Journey Coloring Journals

Sharing the Journey Coloring Journal

Discovery

Reflection

www.ingramcontent.com/pod-product-compliance
Lightning Source LLC
Chambersburg PA
CBHW072108290426
44110CB00014B/1871